DINNER POEMS ©2013 Amanda Montei and Jon Rutzmoser
INTRODUCTION ©2013 Holly Melgard and Joey Yearous-Algozin

ISBN-13: 978-0-615-88072-3

Many thanks to Holly Melgard and Joey Yearous-Algozin. Thanks also to Joe Hall, Anthony
McCann, and Kirsty Singer for their support of this project.

www.bonaireprojects.com

DINNER POEMS

Amanda Montei / Jon Rutzmoser

INTRODUCTION
Holly Melgard / Joey Yearous-Algozin

//
[bon aire projects]

/ INTRODUCTION /

We begin at the scene of collaboration, since *Dinner Poems* takes collaboration as a given.

Here, a line is drawn right down the middle, all the way to the last page of this book. This clean, white streak delineates the center of the page into two columns such that they never touch. Both poets are kept in their place and are forced, even at this formal level, to take sides. Rather than delete this gap, Amanda Montei and Jon Rutzmoser foreground this dividing line in *Dinner Poems*. Perhaps, we can say that their collaborative effort operates on account of this separation, not its resolution.

However, despite the formal regularity of *Dinner Poems*, written each evening at dinner over a 5-month period, precisely naming the boundaries of this collaborative effort proves surprisingly elusive. Titled with only the date of their respective composition, each page is organized into two separate columns justified toward a shared center margin. Each of these columns operate, at times, as independent poems or can be read together, extending or commenting on the other. Take, for instance, this excerpt from "5.1", day two of the project:

he
thinks of
the meat   being
in our hands   in santa's
billowing   lap

Read along its vertical axis, the division of columns distinguishes two separate addresses. Read left to right along the horizontal axis, however, their stylistic indistinctness leaves us with something more perverse: "He thinks of the meat being in our hands, in santa's billowing lap." Either way, we have to ignore one rule to follow another, and throughout the book, we are forced to violate some boundaries to read the poem at all. Still, what interests us here is not so much the book's thematic content or the ambiguity of its poetic address, but the consequences for ourselves as readers in having to choose how to articulate this division.

We could note that this gap is both an irreconcilable dividing line between the two poets, as well as the book's larger, unifying structure and leave it at that. However, in foregrounding the act of collaboration, *Dinner Poems* does not offer this "it's both and neither" solution so easily. Rather than valorizing this ambiguity, the book poses the question of a consistent division running throughout as a problem of the line itself.

Let us explain: Traditionally, the line is what distinguishes poetry from other forms of writing. A line, however, is only recognizable on the basis of its breakage. If the line is a measure or mode of sense, and the only line formed in this book runs down the center, then reading this alignment as *the* common rule of measure becomes an immediate problem.

In "Against Against-isms", written one year after having concluded *Dinner Poems*, Montei rejects the rising trend in discussions of poetry that pose lyric and conceptual modes as competing genres of cerebral and affective style (Jaded Ibis blog, August, 2013). "As a writer whose work actively seeks to disrupt notions of genre," Montei invites an alternative to what she sees as this false ultimatum. Following Montei's assertion of mutual need, "vulnerability" in *Dinner Poems* seems to triangulate a primary locale, or local, between Rutzmoser and Montei.

In light of a desire to re-think genre in terms of compassion and openness, then, we would argue that their respective presence in a text might only be contingent on the relation established between its distributed pronouns. The ambiguity of unspecified authorship unmoors the personal pronouns from their specified locations and objects of desire. *Dinner Poems'* employment of "he" and "she," "we" and "they" statements become self-referential, while the book, simultaneously, sustains a regard for the image of the other. Here, claims made by these historical subjects such as "absent // belly // her torso is / missing /// her arms // her eyes" mark the positioning of a pronoun devoid of an expected specificity, as though "they / could be / anywhere", or, more to the point, anyone. Or, as the manuscript concludes:

> "so   here
>   is where
>   i go in
>   sorry   here
>   is where
>   you do"

Two months after this concluding entry in the manuscript, Rutzmoser continued a similar experiment via Tumblr, inserting private, sensitive information about his identity in the inbox of his email account: In/On "November 13, 2012," Rutzmoser left an email titled *"MY IDENTITY,"* which listed his social security number, date of birth, current address, checking account, check routing number, and mother's maiden name, in his inbox for 12 hours before deleting it.

Similarly, *Dinner Poems* diagrams its subject positions, thus moving collaboration beyond the horizon of a utopian solution. Rather than an insistence on de-centered authorship and communal participation, the articulation of the lyric "I" is flattened onto the printed page. In this way, we read the arrangement of the two columns, justified toward their shared margin, as pointing to the formal categories of the lyric — stanza, line break, and line — as little more than place holders.

Moreover, this occlusion of specific authorship speaks to Bon Aire Projects' stated ethos that "writing is always already a collaborative effort." *Dinner Poems'* success, however, is in spite of this fact. In keeping the individual poems divided on the page, coupled with their refusal to name names, Montei and Rutzmoser co-construct an aesthetic object for whom the author is not dead, but rendered as a generic position in a structural relationship.

Reduced to this almost mathematical logic, Montei and Rutzmoser minimize the formal components of lyric poetry, daybook writing, etc., such that collaboration as an aesthetic category comes to the fore. Perhaps, instead of pursuing the implications, political or otherwise, of its collective identity, *Dinner Poems* forces us to ask: what is collaborative writing as a genre? Moreover, what is the bare minimum at which a genre can function and still be recognized as itself?

Holly Melgard & Joey Yearous-Algozin
Buffalo, NY
2013

/ DINNER POEMS /

for scott / for melissa

4.30

if only
we were   if only
               you were

better   a better
poets   poet

we could   if only
write
a poem   you could
               write
for each   a poem

other   every day

every day

5.01

he fears	i think
the cold	we will
	be alright
rawness	
the exposure	he
	thinks of
the meat	being
in our hands	in santa's
billowing	lap
possibility	his first
	time
the terror	
of consumption	kneeling
	in the
what if	kitchen
our mothers	stink
never stop	arriving
talking	as a
	surprise

5.02

an ache   to bathe
for routine
like a   in your
toothache   dumb
dull and   worm
placeless   noodles
his shadow   to have
hidden   a salt
body crevices   attack
the crooked arm
the back of a knee   i told
you so
the dark   absent
behind her ear   glowing
all giveaways   floating
all   residue
in process   rising
fertile   for the
sake of
she's thought   saying
about embryos   those
but never   dumb
like this   words
never round
and saucy

5.03

she knows	i wonder
eclipsed	deep
that's what	deep
she read	in the
	funk
she likes	
the feeling	my finger
no self	deep
unself	deep
new self	in the
	funk
she likes	
sinking into	a cold
montage	a sore
imagining	
what soundtrack	throat
would play	the wine
at her funeral	just like
imagining	my hand
if there will be	
a eulogy	throat
	onto
this ability	my nipples
to give up	spit in
drive	
towards	the bowl
the image	
the image	head
a virtue	back
	home
to believe	
in drive	funk
is not	somewhere
neurotic	

5.04

<table>
<tr><td></td><td>i smash</td></tr>
<tr><td>the heat</td><td>meat</td></tr>
<tr><td>of other bodies</td><td>with my</td></tr>
<tr><td>radiating inward</td><td>palms</td></tr>
<tr><td>this imbalance</td><td>i fit</td></tr>
<tr><td>this swirling</td><td>more</td></tr>
<tr><td>of shapes</td><td>in my</td></tr>
<tr><td>forms</td><td>mouth</td></tr>
<tr><td>each one</td><td>for you</td></tr>
<tr><td>fracturing</td><td></td></tr>
<tr><td>breaking off</td><td>the pile</td></tr>
<tr><td>on its own</td><td>naked</td></tr>
<tr><td>room</td><td>hairy</td></tr>
<tr><td>like water</td><td>and</td></tr>
<tr><td>she isn't drunk</td><td>ticklish</td></tr>
<tr><td>not yet</td><td>circling</td></tr>
<tr><td>room</td><td>around</td></tr>
<tr><td>turning</td><td>the stick</td></tr>
<tr><td>formless</td><td></td></tr>
<tr><td>open</td><td>the guy</td></tr>
<tr><td>a body</td><td>on tv</td></tr>
<tr><td>is only</td><td>is racist</td></tr>
<tr><td>a container</td><td></td></tr>
<tr><td>after all</td><td>and</td></tr>
<tr><td>the mind</td><td>our</td></tr>
<tr><td>inside</td><td>eyelashes</td></tr>
<tr><td>alone</td><td>touch</td></tr>
<tr><td>screaming</td><td></td></tr>
</table>

5.07

i want
to watch   a man
             saying

365 days
    of spy   words
   movies   words
             words

5.14

here   to cut
he says   off my
              finger

a gap
of time   to float
              in water

here
a spot   is what
that troubles me   we are
              after

missing
the dream   a bottle
the anger   dumb
the reconciliation   dumb cat

her fingers   most of all
are beautiful toe nails
after apologies

5.15

```
                 their back
absent feet      shells
all the time     stretching
    living       and
    without      breaking

                 the weight
how much         from the
                 bird meat
    can we
     know        the juice
                 drips
                 down
    about        their wrists
the other        into
                 the sink
```

5.16

a bad   sisyphus
day   sisyphus

winding   fuck me
up hills   like a
together   hobo

awake   skipping
at dawn   rocks

sniffling   sniffing
purging   concrete
their food

5.18

am i   she asks
a fire   to bend
homeless woman his dick
in flames

            congrats
a cigarette butt
set her
ablaze   after
            a day
you doused me   at work
with coke   he blows
            smoke at
            her naked
sticky   waist line
            an egg shell
i never   spurt in
thank you

5.21

i see
the mom you cry
the bananas and
fantasize
he looks a nose
into her bleeding
eyes
sees her like two
veiled bowls with
tin foil

money
images we'll fall
asleep
communicating washing
their desires ourselves
behind
the wall with static
sea television
of humans
the expectation wanting
of glitter your
red face
there is forever
enough
food this debacle
for everyone

that guy
the guy

5.22

go go   a twin
gadget   named
    justin
i'm   jason
laziness   plays
    paper
my body   rock
plays tricks   scissors
my body   with himself
needs
sooooo much   eyes roll
    backwards
it's   pausing
confused   between
it's   paragraphs
lying   on migrant
    workers
the fat man   suspended
streches   like a
a ring   bridge
sells
chairs   dumb
    lovers
    jump
    together

5.23

i could
smell myself   you ask
all day   if i hear
                        a voice

errupting
volcanoes
they visited   laughing
when she   panicked
was a girl

something about   writing
pele   four words
something about   a minute
a goddess

                        i withdraw
lava   my request

is so
capitalist
                        like
she eats   barren
lava
for breakfast   salmon

5.24

he fears   a white
poetry   corkboard
and all
sauces   for the
     elderly
she fears
he will fuck   not being
someone   able to
else   formulate
     a sentence
don't bend   using
too much   the word
she says   agent
don't give
too much   he
     shoves
she's read   fingers
the internet
     inside
hyphenatation   his eye
is a gap   sockets

a gap
is a place

5.26

like	the
spicy	patriarch
fire	is not
deep fried	dead
	patriarch
oreos	tastes
her insides	
missing	like a
	spirit
prop her up	crackling
like	through
an old lady's	lips
	a sore
his bad	back
back	of the
	throat

5.27

```
                    your
                    body
        tonight     flips
        carnage     in the air
             is     it is not

disproportionate    thanksgiving
        lacking     your
                    mother
    a wooden
        person      no longer

    wide eyed       calls you
                    charlie
                    brown
    glistening
                    oh no
                    now
                    she only
                    calls
                    to cry
```

5.28

the dirty
dozen

bugs   crawling
or war   on
       your
       chest
they forgot
       you
she did eat watch
a bug once puppets
in college on tv

big buckets hoping
of glass you'll
      tickle
      me
feelings

5.29

a pedant
rubbing oil cuts his
feet
eyes bow-tied
half closing throat
next to

i want a smiling
monk
to be
a bad father
happy poet yoga
in hot
not pants
a good
sad one listening to
"conceptual"
or ungainly
"colloborative" voices
or "installation" in the world

"something" clambering
about
in the
"future"

5.30

an ice pack
on his head   you're fat
    you feel

blood pooling

    your back
the world   smelling
crying   your own
    feet

wedding
marriage   you know
concept   i work hard

two dumb   you know
young people   that fish
accidentally   is done
    right

have
an iphone
app   you know
    nothing

5.31

"two halves   lost in
             walmart
  make
two halves" you are
             wearing
  she saw a swimsuit
  human
    shit "wanna fuck?"
  today
  a man meows
sneezed outside
  on her
          "what is
she felt ours
wetness is ours"

she felt

         you spit
feelings on my
         love handle
  about
bow ties

6.04

her mother
put out   a coin toss
cold spaghetti   a sheetless
                 bed
for guests
                 it's a
brain matter   kind of
                 plastic
peeled grapes   jobless
like eyes   love

attached   forever
to other things a sidekick
                 despite
a thing-life   market
                 values
alone
and wet   your
                 asshole
                 the dishes

6.05

he says	a boy
that's poetic	in a
	welding mask
he says	stares
	up at
dehydrated	sun
she's nervous	this idiot
or thinking	will
	someday
	be
very hard	
	a science teacher
about	
bodies	driving
she writes	a fear of
a love poem	gravity
on his forehead	
	it is
	not that
something	
changes	everyone
	is wrong

6.07

i want
to watch   you look
            at photos
the end
            of children
you want   parents
to know

a bride   it's late
insomia   we want
a caretaker to fuck
anxiety   to watch
a fetus's   house
            but
discontent the season
            is over
i'm not sure the interview
            is over
if there
are lines   schizophrenic
here   boys
if there
is more   over
here   and
            over
i'm fat
i like it

6.08

just fucked
in old age   a vibrator
they'll have
sex parties   my feet
are sore
not because   my arms
they're good   scratched
from
special   remembering
the guy
they like   screaming
a challenge   about our
communist
body   book
parts   at the
post office
so many
surfaces   anarchy
anarchy

they   the women
still   oppose it
know
nothing   stinking of
a magic
eraser

6.11

i am

paper not happy
penises with you
flanking
the bed you say
she thinks knocking
on the door

about
representation a slice
of pizza

she sucked
a dick lollipop moving back
to new york

confections laughing
are about
the huge
inability
to say no less
traumatic
than expected

how long
will they leave a giant
a penis
in the fridge the first
power plant
in los angeles

she sucked
a dick a girl's
lollipop best friend
the king
will burn

desire
dead

6.13

it was   a strange
a terrible day hand
at the races   combing
              the cat
so they left   on a
              plane

the poor
animal   if he
behind   doesn't
              know
              then
              fuck him

7.04

tonight spongy flesh
i ate in his mouth
a heart

he devours it

the horizon
lit up "today is
with the taste a throw away
aluminum day"
riddled with he says

spelling errors "where do I
get
a new one?"

independents'
day
for example

7.05

three weeks
tomorrow

sometimes
the weight   the boxes
           the heavy

induces
hiccups   heavy

she tries   nothing
to catch
her breath   and the
tiny   little
lung   blast of
        salt
shrinks   coughs
        out

soon
she thinks   "spell
        potato"
i'll be

so small   asshole
i'll echo

7.06

the vest	asleep
has five	teeth
buttons	clenched
the voice	her wine
muffled	spilling
and or	onto
belly up	her bare chest
in your	
monster	she is
arms	the world
	the pillow
	her mouth

7.07

she sedates	the dead
herself	his ashes
to sleep	somewhere
	the dried
ecological	piss
preserve	on the
imagining	floor
being trapped	
in a car	uniformed
for 6 days	people
	spray
she can feel	poison
her teeth	on toes
chewing	pushing
	cars

7.08

we argue   the tasks
            repeated
i picture
        you keeping track
             learning
downward
      dog people ask
     sniff the same
            questions
rice boils

            maybe
paper wads she'll learn
   stuffed top stitch
in nostrils eat s'mores

            ward off
 laughing bears

  through and then
 sickness repeat

            ask someone

            repeat

7.09

you	
remind me	there is
boxes	a hollowing
the phone	that occurs
ringing	maybe
on our	fear
walk	or just
pick a	
card	absence
send it	
	she says
i want	
to say	but she
the book	is not sure
i need	
the dates	what means
listed	forgetting
in order	what means
but what	not
i need	an option
what	
we need	she sweats
is	herself
	sick
less	fear
	and
	joy
	is
	hard

7.12

eating sand   the healthy
                 cat screams
the way
the girl   sick
does   as though
a pregnant   dying
woman   in his own
images   cage
of him   jaundiced
as a boy
fat   not
squat   knowing
            the voice
the possibility   telling
of wanting   the man
            just breathe
one day
they will meet   as she pulls
a young   thick red
boy or girl   from him

it will
scream   he is
           used
           to it

7.13

a dumb child
sings   a
happy   wedding
birthday   on her
to a   birthday
dead
cockroach

      she throws
two   cake
lovers   in the bride's
kiss   face
on a roof
crouching   then steals
as if they   her flowers
are wrestlers

7.18

he forgoes
the internet   lawnmowers
blessing   blowing
                     bubbles

they walk
across
the border   bullies
for tamales   he thinks
                     white wine

fully licensed
they contemplate   bleached
state   teeth
guards
documents   the state
complicity   said yes

                     there will be
bad Marxists   no fish
they enjoy it   no bodies
                     no water

7.19

"crocodile
rock"
love for
everything   the balloons
have dresses
shiny   lack
bubbles   nothing

children   he shushes her
as if
the girl   a poem
with curls   is anything
without
interruptions
sleeping
on a bed
of grass   as if he
they hand mow   is anything

painting   tomorrow
they mail
tomorrow   money
they will finish
the curtain   the fleas
with fringe   won't bite
she will
miss   if there's
a god
the little girl

7.23

it's   her teeth
an oil
change   the hills
            the meeting spot
            for grumbling men
enjoy
            he lets her
a sigh   rest
across   on his shoulder
an extra
night   the matriarch
            in the airfield
a plane asks
            "what
fucking vow
mark   are you
            taking?"
napping
for hours suspended
            a crane
forever full of sand
            emptying
those   on her
letters
            she holds
            her breath
            she tastes
            the grit

7.24

a child   in the
screaming   morning
"no!"   a small boy
                 dances
everything
happens   they smell
                 eggs
the game   his favorite
of fake   word
baseball
                 "no"
                 she tries
he pretends   to make him
to be   say "yes"
before us
                 a woman
i want   brands her
you under
my armpit   "i <3 j"

our waitress   her skin
thinking   peeling
only
one thing

7.25

a view
of the beach   he meets
she talks   her twin
about nursing   they hug
in salty air

what kind

nice to
glorifying   see you
free soap
the evil twin   nice to
looking on   sit in
traffic

they pack in
and eat   a dirty
unawkward   car game

the tall man   they do
reveals   their best
himself   to please

friendly   fuck you
and giving   mickey
mouse

light
and water

7.26

spell   free
pasta   coffee
      a walk
      on the beach

speak
to people   a boy
      learning

"thank you
for coming"   i worry
"thank you   a tree
for this   this is
all-occasion   the mark
candle"

      drink
she's   face first
lost   in the ocean
her sweater

      the rocketeer
the little boy   hovering
crying

      jesus

they don't
eat cake

7.27

```
                  he waits
the little boy    exactly
                  one year

   mini pies

                  one year
two sisters       give or
                  take

on a beach
no money           sleepless
for juice          freedom
                   day

the noise
of dresses        to write
                  a poem
   swish           for her
   swish

                  great
bubbles           scott
the little boy's
bow tie           paper
the children      paper
on a field trip
men crying        paper
```

7.28

her belly   the headache
a tree   the headache
her belly   the omelette
a hillside   the omelette
an oversized
balloon   two boys
   running
decorated   on lawn
   chairs
floating
   the water
unassuming   the hot tub
guests
let go   you sleep
too easy   beside
   the blonde
a fake candle   say bye
burns   with cake
the little boy   in a box
grows up
   the cake
blows it out   in the box
   we'll forget
the mother   her metal back
weeps

7.29

	looking
no room	for neon
to recline	they find
	a small
dresser	hot town
and bed	
on the	suicide
sidewalk	
	chicken
an air	sandwich
conditioner	sex
alone	tired faces
in a	smoking
triangular	inside
room	
	ghostbusters
jackpot	batman
	wine
they wait	hidden
in line	behind
watching	frames
girls	
drink	open road
tequila	towards Canada
go usa	the derby girl
	crosses the road
the world	
the oysters	a strange
	easy
	goodbye

7.30

bad timing
leaving   change
for good   in his pocket

he pitches   she shakes
a tent   and sweats

chocolate   he feels
on her palms desperate

the old man   blowing
snoring   embers

              they
              could be
              anywhere

7.31

sign reads:
"i am   the guy
inaudible"   stumbling
               slapping
a reservation my face
roadside stand

               the navajo
an embrace   places them
               on a list
"there is
nothing   we play
out here"   truck driver
               and whore
she might
have said   a beetle
               crawls
but didn't
               in circles
driving back   the car
forth   the coffee
back   the shower
forth   takes
in gray mountain knuckle
               grease
the family
wordless   tourists
signing   welcome

montei / rutzmoser

8.01

the city
slicker
photographs   gray
   gasless
fire   they race
ants   on stationary
climb up   bikes
his pants

   eat vegan
rock   sandwiches
balance

   snap photos
   of that wagon

she updates
her status
three times   "is this the
   pretty part?"

"the sun
won't set"   the forest burns
   the fall
"show   will kill us
me
your   scenes
manchops"   of melancholy

he   speaks
photographs   to a mouse
her

8.02

no

she eats free
farm-raised shit
fish
and cream a sign
a city
named this is not
after what they
murdered expected
animals

medicinal
maybe doc
we could holiday
find someone eating
happy dirt
for us

she's
a sick girl happy
holding fabric
her father's eyes
hand
a sulfur styrofoam
smell worms
between
fat tiny faces
men
fat the weirdness
women of a century
in love
they steal
vanishing robes

8.03

"give me   people
a man   touch us
as big as   in fake oceans
mountains"

                this town
                smells
he's   like farts
pissing   i love it
the ideology
of a mountain   shaving
a man   in public
or pork   i love you
                pork
a pig   watermelon
punishing   i love arugula
little children
with   i love
coffee   everything
a pig   that's worth
smoking $100
cigars
while   our lives
roasting   the velcro
                ripping
salt him   my penis

8.04

he sat   just
in gum   passing
he says through
says it
again   a mountain
        my blood
"i think on it
i sat   years ago
in gum" that man
he's   in the shell
so sad

        millions of
"you are bikers
landlocked wake up!
don't eat that shadow!
fish"

        look at
reenacting my
prohibition cup
in a hotel of spittle

both doors i made it
work   for you
well   while
        you
women were sleeping
circling

        kansas
"it   welcomed us
isn't cheap" i shit
he says

shame	near-death
fisting	things
honeybuns	she says
muffins and	imagining
coffee	her eyes
	peering
they wait	through
in line	an arch
to taste	
smoke	the man's
	voice
she is	the logisitics
angry	of eating
slamming	too much
waste	rice
in a	
waste can	also
the gas	waiting
station	too long
closed	for
	the toilet
the tall boy	the skunk
in the cup	smell of
the car	the tough kid
on its head	
	the convenience
dangling	store
from	closed
a seat belt	but everyone
she says	is cheering
her name	
she says	the skyline
she can't	
move	she can't
	focus
i make	on anything
	but
small talk	his face

8.06

i want to
try it
all ways
not-quite
southern
jazz
and
i want
to practice
a dance
with kicks

going to
the place
like
the other
place

he can't
get
on top

they
go back
for more
on a
stone bench
watch
people in
red

the little boy
the little girl
the flower
in her hair

food kills
stop eating

the pillowtop
sleeps
changing

backwards
the cat
shitting in
new places
the old
couple
their
dollar menu

a free
cup
of water
rolls off
the car
in reverse

he yells
at her
sleeping

he wants to
stare
into her
vagina

to have
a soul

8.08

they refuse
teleology   sometimes
process   it's better
                 to walk
on the dash   she says
a voice

"just drive"

8.09

they christen
the bed
i don't think   but she
we should   does not
you say

her mother
a dishrag   losing her job
for drying   her mother
hands   gaining a
therapist

the beeping
the heat   you cannot
finish
the new   my sentences

teeth   discounts
whitening   a lamp post
commercial   a yellow sign

a park   they fear
a street   they'll never
read

8.10

he
finishes   she
too   gives him
soon   too
little

8.11

driving   his mother's
feet
tangled
his mom   in tubes
in the hospital   the little boy
beats
a balloon
her husband's
knees   waiting
for
visiting hours
she asks   to end
the doctor for   jell-o
her metal spine   is alive

she wants   a nurse
to go home   young
tending to
kill   blood sugar
the cat   everyone
watching

a cage
the sound
of a nail gun   "a pocket book"
children
screaming   it is hard
working
he'll cry   backwards

searching now   the home
for the   now dry
light switch

8.14

	the cyborg
bed bug	gets hard
eating	wrestling
mac	with
n chz	the girl
under-poured	fisting
glasses	chocolate
wine	curtain
cold	truffles
	oh god
the kind	
of place	dr. joe
news vans	
visit	fat and
	awkward
bites	
all over	rubbing
her body	sticks
the view	together
the feeling	to make
of looking	a pretzel
the feeling	a blushing
forward	canadian
tomorrow	they drink
they bathe	to his
in the mist	daughter
of the falls	
something	
salty	whitewash
in the water	in june
moving	the blowjob
like	the two
not moving	sisters
	anderson
	cooper

8.15

she
imagines   the falls
one day   falling
he throws   look
a fork   at us
at her

    ponchos
a bottomless   spit
    on our toes

like people
with cameras   oatmeal
    from doctors'
she overhears   trash cans

she can't   we all want
recognize   to wake
tells him   to watch
she wants   dumb
    sci-fi films

knowing

    smell
she makes him   coffee
miserable

    strangers
they register
for   mostly
a library card

    we want
hope   our cat
for them   to shut
    the fuck up

8.16

women   blinking
don't have
much   her toes
time   her knees

oh sigh
               they
two keys   wonder if
in a carboard
envelope   they'll ever
               be able
               to sit
carrot
puree   comfortably
on a large
lenox
christmas
plate   they eat
               like
               toddlers

8.18

the city   a vietnamese
cowboy
is closed   doing
sunday   push ups

cans   for the jobless
in carts   in the city
could pay
our rent   let's just
forget
the bride   causality
checks
her phone   and spit
in the wind

drowns   on her way
to do something
a spider
a gift card
dead   at walmart
women
in hoop skirts   so sorry
looking   to disappoint

8.19

<pre>
                today
her sister
    is a   is
                missing
character
    too   what
            is he
            after
</pre>

8.20

the metal back
of an
old car

you are
a character

too

8.21

buckwheat
makes
a difference

dextrose
doesn't make
a difference
i think

your
ebay
account

your
embarrassment

i once
pictured
you living
inside
of me
she said

you and your
underwear

you will be
a citizen
again

his father
his mother's
vacuum
buckwheat
for a brain

in a bag
so much
worrying

and he
smacks
her ass

praying

she'll know
his way

like a cat
meowing
at a mirror

screaming
jumping
under
the bed

with her

8.22

someone
saying   he writes
something   one sentence
about   7,000
              times

their
state   dedicates it
being   to the man
              within
"talk
to me"   she may
              not be
he never   embarrassed
used enough
salt   he may
              not be
"there aren't
enough   masturbating
lists
in the world" swallowing
              a shot gun
yellow
papers   fucking
on stairs   hippie
              fucking
the mother   tree
listening to hugger
love songs
the little boy hugs
valorizing the 7,000
cat   trees

the one
with the sore
behind
his ear

8.26

thirsty
absent
what will
sustain   belly
us

           her torso is
not   missing
organic
lettuce

           her arms
not
free range   her eyes
hormone
free   useless
busy

just   rain
           quiet
don't   in this
           city
worry

           the water
must
be soft

8.27

```
                        "you don't
          make          know
          meaning       the cost
          she says      of culture"


        "we gotta
         look out       "it has been
             for        7,000 days
      each other"       since
                        i lost
            love        my virginity"


          poem          she blames
                        mysticism
       "the truth
        of it all       she
                        pictures
          is that       him
          in this       cradling
            game        a rabbit
          of life       explaining
     we're a team"
                        she thinks
            look
            out!        al gore


           chuck        his song
           chuck        the car
          bobuck        speeding


                        a queue
                        mourning
                        the loss
```

8.28

not
looking for somewhere
transcendence in echo park
only a poet
a name has the flu
for letters

her happiness
for that is crucial
half can
of beans

the man
the boy at the
paper hat library
listening
eating to big band
french fries

more than
famous

she goes
there her brain
wrinkling
signs his socks
her name dirty
the trash
the little can
boy
makes a spider
rice crispie "no spider"
treats she says
for his mother i will not
dance
too much with your
eight legs

8.29

what could
be called
an encyclopedia

over
there
ness

modernism
like

"hey
where
did you
go?"

waiting
in line
at the dmv

he
wants
to kiss

like
photographing
a coin

the kitchen

the little boy

a kiss
in the kitchen
foreign
bookstore

the mother
an open
pessimist
feminist

their sofa
is modern
cardboard

whenever
she has
to wait

no
he tells her

their eyes
all judgey
and watery

standing in

she draws
them

the doorway

a diagram

so

"here
is where
i go in

sorry

here
is where
you do"

www.ingramcontent.com/pod-product-compliance
Lightning Source LLC
Chambersburg PA
CBHW060419050426
42449CB00009B/2039